MW01141649

SANGUDO PUBLIC LIBRARY
BOX 524
SANGUDO, AB T0E 2A0

DISCOVERING PAINTINGS

MYTHS & LEGENDS

Anne Civardi

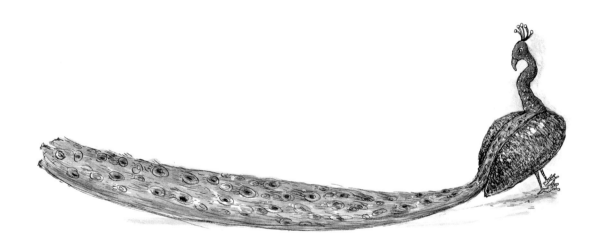

SANGUDO PUBLIC LIBRARY
BOX 524
SANGUDO, AB T0E 2A0

Chrysalis Education
in association with The National Gallery, London

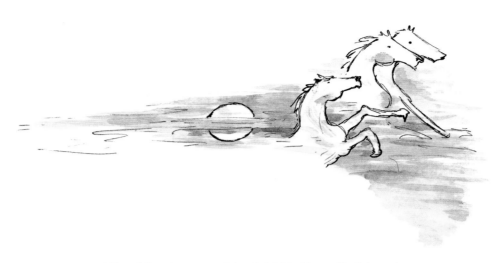

US publication copyright © 2003 Chrysalis Education

International copyright reserved in all countries.
No part of this book may be reproduced in any form
without written permission from the publisher.

Distributed in the United States by
Smart Apple Media,
1980 Lookout Drive
North Mankato, Minnesota 56003

Copyright © Chrysalis Books PLC 2003
Text © Anne Civardi & Ruth Thomson 2003
Illustrations © National Gallery Company Limited 2003
From an original idea created by National Gallery Company, 2001,
which was generously supported by Mr. and Mrs. Anthony Speelman

ISBN 1 93198 368 2

The Library of Congress control number 2003102566

Editorial manager: Joyce Bentley
Consultant: Erika Langmuir
Educational consultant: Hector Doyle
Design: Mei Lim
Illustrator: Serena Feneziani
Project manager for National Gallery Company: Jan Green

Printed in China

Contents

About this book

The pictures chosen for this book are all based on captivating stories: myths about Ancient Greek or Roman gods and heroes, and legends from the Bible. The word "myth" comes from the Greek "muthos" meaning story, while "legend" comes from the Latin for "that which is to be read."

The picture of *Tobias and the Angel,* for example, is part of a story from the Apocrypha, an appendix to the Bible, written about 200 years before the birth of Christ. When artists paint stories from the past, they often set them in their own times. Verrocchio lived in Italy in the fifteenth century where young men like Tobias often wore dashing, embroidered clothes and curled their hair.

The painting of *Apollo and Daphne* shows a dramatic moment from a Greek myth. The artist lived in Florence during an exciting time for painters, known as the Renaissance—which means "rebirth." Renaissance painters were inspired by myths and legends from Ancient Rome and Greece. Rather than painting mainly religious pictures of Christian saints and stories from the Bible, Renaissance artists began to turn also to the writings of Ancient Greek and Roman authors.

Many of these, such as Homer's tale of the massive Wooden Horse built by the Greeks to defeat the Trojans in a legendary war, continued to inspire artists in later centuries, as you can see in the two magnificent pictures by Tiepolo on page 29.

Ways of telling a story

Although paintings like these can show only frozen moments in a story, artists use all sorts of techniques to help you work out what might have happened before that moment and what might happen next. The most important people in a story are often placed in the center or in the foreground of the painting, and may be more brilliantly lit than everyone else. Their facial expressions, poses, positions, or gestures may tell you how they are feeling and suggest what they have just done or are about to do. Look for these clues as you explore each picture.

Using this book

This book focuses on six main paintings based on a myth or legend. There are four sections about each picture that will help you to find out more about it.

 asks questions about the painting, which can all be answered by looking at certain details.

 suggests activities that involve your senses and your imagination.

 gives background information about the painting and includes answers to some of the *Look Closer* questions.

 provides another painting on a similar theme for you to compare and contrast with the first one.

Tobias and the Angel

(1470 – 80)

Attributed to Andrea del Verrocchio

A young boy called Tobias was sent on a journey to collect some money owed to his blind father. On his travels, Tobias was joined by the Archangel Raphael, who had been sent to protect him. This picture tells the story of their journey.

 **LOOK CLOSER**

What clues tell you that Tobias' companion is an angel?

Do you think Tobias and the angel are friends?
How can you tell?

Look at Tobias' left hand and the angel's left hand.
Do you notice anything strange about them?

What is the angel holding in his right hand?
What is Tobias holding in his left hand?

Can you spot a little dog somewhere in the picture?
(Clue: it is almost transparent.)

 TAKE ACTION

Imagine that you are traveling with Tobias and the Angel. **What dangers might the three of you have experienced on your journey?** Think about the people and animals you might meet.

Explain why you think you would feel safe if the Archangel Raphael accompanied you on a long journey to a faraway city.

Find four similarities between Tobias and the Angel. Find four differences by looking at color, shape, and line.

If you could touch the objects in the picture, how would each one feel?
- hard
- soft
- wet
- hairy
- silky
- cold
- slimy
- furry

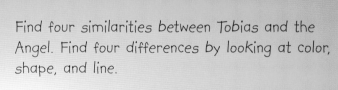

A Guardian Angel

One day, Tobias set off with his dog to travel to a faraway city to collect the money owed to his blind father. On the way, he was attacked and nearly eaten by a monstrous fish. The Archangel Raphael, disguised as a fellow traveler, told Tobias to catch the fish and cut out its heart, liver, and gall bladder. The gall bladder would cure his father's blindness.

The picture on page 6 shows Tobias carrying the body of the dead fish, while the angel holds its heart, liver, and gall bladder in a small wooden box. When they returned home, the angel explained that Tobias' father's eyesight would be restored as soon as he rubbed the fish's gall bladder over his blind eyes.

This picture was painted in Florence over 500 years ago, when traveling was very dangerous. Florentines had a particular devotion to the Archangel Raphael, since many of their young men, like Tobias, went abroad on business. Paintings such as this helped to reassure those at home that their sons or husbands would also enjoy the angel's protection.

 **LOOK FURTHER**

Tobias and the Archangel Raphael returning with the Fish (MID – 17TH CENTURY)
After Adam Elsheimer

This picture was painted 300 years later than the one on page 6. It concentrates more on the landscape and less on the story of the Archangel protecting Tobias.

The figures are placed to one side so that you can see into the far distance. Look at the size of the fish Tobias is dragging. What other differences can you spot?

Does this picture seem more or less realistic than Verrocchio's? Why?

What distinguishes the angel from an ordinary person?

Does the painting feel noisy or quiet to you? What makes you say that?

What do you think the Angel might be saying to Tobias as they walk along?

9

Apollo and Daphne

(PROBABLY 1470 – 80)

Antonio del Pollaiuolo

This curious picture was painted over 500 years ago. It tells the story of Apollo, the Greek god of the sun, who fell in love with a beautiful nymph named Daphne. Something very strange happened to Daphne when she asked her father, a river god, to help her escape from Apollo's clutches.

LOOK CLOSER

Can you *see* a winding river in the background?
Why do you think the artist has included it?

Pollaiuolo has used different colors to give a sense of distance.
How do the colors in the foreground differ
from those in the background?

Do you think Daphne looks afraid of Apollo?

In the painting, Apollo is smiling.
Do you think he will be smiling for long? Why not?

What colors has the artist used to make Apollo and Daphne
stand out from the background?

How can you tell that Apollo has been running?
(Clue: look at his clothes.)

TAKE ACTION

Ask a friend to help you make up a story
to fit the picture. One person starts, reaches
an exciting moment, and then lets the other
person take over.

Imagine you are Daphne's father,
the river god, with magical powers.
**What might you have done to help your
daughter get away from Apollo?**

What kind of tree do you think Daphne
has turned into?

Ask a friend to stand with you just like the
two people in the painting. Now imagine the
conversation they might *be* having.
• **Do you think Daphne is cross with Apollo?**
• **Do you think Apollo is trying to persuade
Daphne to become his lover?**

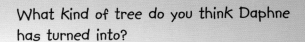

Apollo's Tree of Love

In the Greek myth, Apollo fell in love with Daphne when he was struck in the heart with a sharp, gold-tipped arrow fired by Cupid. To make sure that Daphne never fell in love with Apollo, Cupid pierced her heart with a lead-tipped shaft.

Apollo begged Daphne to be his love but, unable to bear the thought of giving up her freedom, she ran away from him, deep into the forest. Just as Apollo was about to catch her, Daphne asked her father (a river god) to save her by opening up the earth or changing her form entirely. Instantly, her toes turned to roots, her fingers to twigs, and bark covered her body as she was transformed into a laurel tree.

Grief-stricken that Daphne had escaped his grasp, Apollo vowed to worship the tree she had become and always to wear a wreath made from its leaves on his head. In ancient times, laurel wreaths were worn as a mark of honor in memory of the myth of Apollo and Daphne.

 **LOOK FURTHER**

Apollo pursuing Daphne
(1616 – 18) **Domenichino and Assistants**

This picture of Apollo and Daphne by Domenichino is painted in a very different style from the one on page 10.

It was originally painted on the wall of a palace in Italy. How many similarities can you spot between the two paintings?

Do you think Daphne looks more frightened of Apollo than she does in the painting by Pollaiuolo?
How would you describe the expression on her face?

Daphne looks as if she might be calling for help.
Whom do you think she might be calling to?

How does the background differ from the one on page 10?

Bacchus and Ariadne

(1522 – 3) **Titian**

This painting shows the moment when Ariadne, a brave
and beautiful princess, meets Bacchus (the god of wine)
and his noisy followers. Ariadne has been abandoned
on an island by her lover, a hero called Theseus.

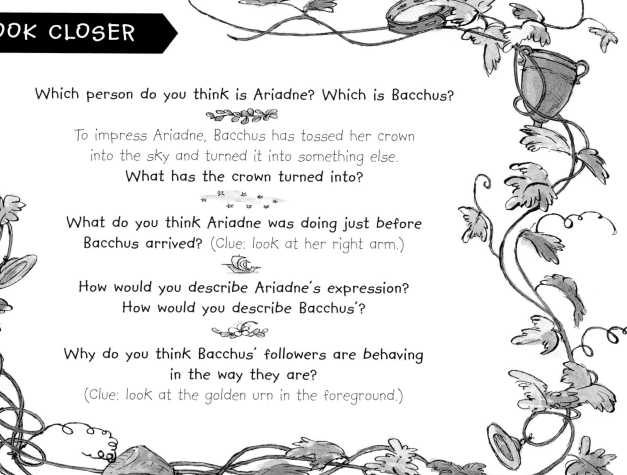

Which person do you think is Ariadne? Which is Bacchus?

To impress Ariadne, Bacchus has tossed her crown
into the sky and turned it into something else.
What has the crown turned into?

What do you think Ariadne was doing just before
Bacchus arrived? (Clue: look at her right arm.)

How would you describe Ariadne's expression?
How would you describe Bacchus'?

Why do you think Bacchus' followers are behaving
in the way they are?
(Clue: look at the golden urn in the foreground.)

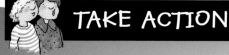

TAKE ACTION

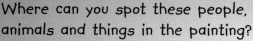

Where can you spot these people,
animals and things in the painting?
- the head and leg of a calf
- two musical instruments
- two people other than Bacchus and
  Ariadne who are looking at each other
- Theseus' ship sailing away
- four different kinds of animals
- a very drunk man
- a satyr (someone who is half-human
  and half-goat)

Pretend you are standing next to Ariadne.
What sounds might you hear around you?

Titian is famous for the bright, glowing colors
in his paintings.
- How many colors can you see?
- Which colors are the brightest?
- Which two colors link Ariadne
  with Bacchus?

Ariadne's Story

Before she met Bacchus, Ariadne had been in love with a hero called Theseus. She agreed to help him kill a terrible monster, the Minotaur, who lived in a dark labyrinth and ate girls and boys, as long as Theseus promised to take her away with him.

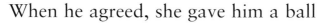

When he agreed, she gave him a ball of string. While Ariadne held one end of the string, Theseus crept through the labyrinth, leaving a trail of string behind him. Before long, he came face to face with the hideous beast and with one giant blow, he killed it. Then he followed the string back to his loving Ariadne. They sailed away to the distant island of Naxos.

While Ariadne was fast asleep, Theseus left without her. The poor princess woke just in time to see his ship disappearing into the distance. As she wandered along the shore, she heard clashing cymbals, laughing, and barking. Bacchus, the god of wine, had arrived with his friends. As soon as he saw Ariadne, Bacchus fell deeply in love with her. He loved her so much that his wedding present to her was the sky. He took her crown and hurled it into the sky, where it turned into a crown of twinkling stars.

 **LOOK FURTHER**

Bacchus and Ariadne
(PROBABLY 1700 – 10) **Sebastiano Ricci**

Compare this picture of Bacchus and Ariadne with the one by Titian on page 14. It shows a much more peaceful meeting between the two lovers.

Ariadne has not yet woken to find that Theseus has left her and sailed away from the island of Naxos. What other differences can you spot?

Which person do you think is Bacchus?

What do you think is in the golden urn at the bottom left of the picture? Why do you think it is included in the painting? (Clue: think about why Bacchus' followers are so merry and rowdy.)

How will Ariadne feel when she wakes up?

The Judgment of Paris

(ABOUT 1600)

Peter Paul Rubens

This picture shows the moment when Paris, a prince disguised as a shepherd, ends an argument between three goddesses—Juno, Minerva, and Venus. He is asked to choose the most beautiful by giving her a golden apple.

LOOK CLOSER

Which one is Paris? What is he holding?

Do you think Paris has decided which goddess to choose?

Minerva, the Goddess of Wisdom, has a shield.
Can you find her?

Venus, the Goddess of Love, has a baby son, Cupid,
who carries a bow and quiver of arrows.
Can you spot him and his mother?

Juno is the Queen of all the Gods and Goddesses.
Her symbol is the peacock.
Can you find her?

Mercury, the Messenger of the Gods, is wearing a winged helmet.
Where can you see him in the picture?

TAKE ACTION

Which one of the three goddesses would you choose if you were Paris? Why? Would it be because of her beauty, or perhaps because of the bribe she has offered you (see page 20)?

Apart from Minerva, Venus, and Juno, there is one other goddess.
• Can you find her?

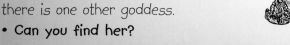

Imagine what Mercury might by saying as he stands next to his friend Paris.

Two of the goddesses both think that they have won, while the other knows she has not.
• **Can you see which is which?**
(Clue: look at their hands and feet.)

• **Can you spot four different kinds of animal in the painting?**
Make the noises you might expect each animal to make.

The Capture of the Golden Fleece

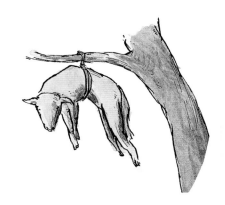

(1742 – 3) **Jean-François Detroy**

Based on an ancient Greek myth, this intriguing picture shows the moment when Jason and his brave companions, the Argonauts, capture the Golden Fleece. Medea, a sorceress who fell in love with Jason, helped him in his dangerous quest.

LOOK CLOSER

Which one is Jason? What is he doing?
How would you describe the expression on his face?

What do you think is guarding the Golden Fleece?

Which one is Medea?
Why do you think Medea is gesturing towards the dragon?

Do you think the dragon looks dead or asleep?

This painting was used as a design for a big tapestry.
For this reason, the artist did not need to include much
detail and painted it in a sketchy style.
What parts of the painting look most sketchy?

TAKE ACTION

Look at the picture for 60 seconds.
Now look away.
How many things can you remember?

What do you think might have
happened just before the moment
shown in the picture?

How did Jason travel to the land where
the Golden Fleece was kept?

What kind of person do you imagine
Jason to be?

- handsome
- strong
- a good leader
- brave
- foolish
- rash

What kind of person do you imagine
Medea, the sorceress, to be?

- kind
- cunning
- friendly
- cruel
- gentle
- loving

23

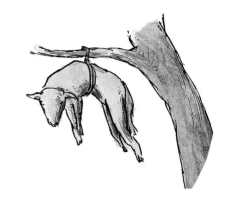

Jason and the Argonauts

The Golden Fleece that Jason was sent to capture was made of pure gold. It had been stripped from a magical ram and taken to Colchis. In exchange for returning it to his uncle, Pelias, King of Iolcus, in Thessaly, Jason was to be given back the throne that was rightfully his.

During Jason and the Argonauts' quest to capture the fleece, they had to perform many difficult tasks. First they had to sail through jagged, clashing rocks and whirlpools. Then, when they arrived at Colchis, the King there made them plow a field with fire-breathing bulls and sow dragons' teeth into the earth. Immediately, ferocious warriors sprang up from the ground. Jason and his men defeated them in a tough battle.

Medea, the king's daughter who loved Jason, helped him in all these tasks. She led him to where the Golden Fleece was guarded by a huge, hissing dragon. She sneaked up to it, sang a soothing lullaby, and put it to sleep with her magic potion. Jason quickly snatched the Golden Fleece and sailed home to Thessaly with Medea.

Jason married Medea but left her for another woman many years later. Medea was so angry that she killed all their children as well as his new wife.

LOOK FURTHER

Jason Swearing Eternal Affection to Medea (1742 – 3) **Jean-François Detroy**

This picture, also by Jean-François Detroy, shows the moment when Jason tells the sorceress, Medea, how much he loves her and begs her to help him. In return, he promises to marry her.

Behind them is an ancient stone altar dedicated to Hecate, a goddess linked with sorcery. The artist has used similar colors in both paintings. What other similarities can you spot?

Do you think Jason really loves Medea or that he just wants her help?

Do you think Medea really loves Jason?

Who do you think the winged figures are? What are they about to do? Why?

Medea is giving Jason magic herbs. **What might their juice be used for?** (Clue: remember what happened to the dragon that guarded the Golden Fleece.)

Ulysses deriding Polyphemus

(1829)

J.M.W. Turner

Imagine that, like Ulysses in this painting, you and your men are sailing home from the Trojan War. Tired and hungry, you stop off at an island to look for food. Suddenly you come face to face with Polyphemus, a ferocious one-eyed giant. How do you make your escape?

LOOK CLOSER

Do you think Ulysses' ship is sailing away
from the land or just passing it by?

Do you think Ulysses is anxious to leave quickly?
Give the reasons for your answer.
(Clue: have all the sails of his ship *been* unfurled?
Have all the oars been pushed out of the oar holes yet?)

Which person do you think is Ulysses?
What color is he wearing that makes him stand out?

What can you *see* swimming in front of the ship?

How has the artist given us a sense of drama?
(Clue: look at the colors used and the action in the picture.)

TAKE ACTION

The artist has painted Polyphemus
somewhere in the picture.
Where is he?

Imagine what it would be like to be one
of the crew on Ulysses' ship.
- **What are the conditions like
  on board?**
- **What is your job?**
- **How are you feeling?**

Which of the following words best
describe the mood of the painting?
- exciting
- frantic
- dangerous
- serene
- calm
- jolly
- threatening
- mysterious

Look at the rising sun. Turner has scraped
some animal outlines into the wet paint.
- **What are they? (See page 28.)**

The One-eyed Giant

In the story, Ulysses and his men were unaware that the island they had landed on was the home of the Cyclopes—man-eating giants with one huge eye in the middle of their foreheads.

Before long, the warriors came across a cave filled with cheese and milk. As they were hungrily eating the food, the owner of the cave returned—it was Polyphemus. Furious to find them there, the giant attacked and ate two of Ulysses' men. The following day he devoured two more.

That night, Ulysses heated a sharpened stake in a fire and plunged it into the sleeping giant's eye, blinding him. Then the hero devised a very cunning trick. As Polyphemus herded his sheep out of the cave, the warriors hung on to the sheep's bellies so that the giant would not be able to feel them. Escaping back to their ship, they sailed away.

The artist did not want any of the magical figures in the painting to be easily recognized. He has disguised Polyphemus as a moutain top and made the spirits of the sea look like waves in front of Ulysses' ship. He has also made it difficult to spot the horses of the sun god, Apollo, painted just above the rising sun.

LOOK FURTHER

(top) The Building of the Trojan Horse
(bottom) The Procession of the Trojan Horse into Troy
(1760) **Giovanni Domenico Tiepolo**

During the Trojan War, the Greeks made a huge, hollow wooden horse to hide their soldiers inside and attack Troy. One of these soldiers was Menelaus, the husband of Helen of Troy, whose elopement with Paris started the war.

The Greeks left the horse outside the walls of Troy and waited for the Trojans to pull it into the city. Then they jumped out, attacked, and defeated the Trojans. These two pictures describe that part of the Tojan War.

Ulysses and his men had taken part in the Trojan war before they came across Polyphemus, and may well be in the top painting.
What do you think Ulysses might be doing? Which of these people might he be?

Does the horse look wooden or real? Is it big enough for the soldiers to hide inside?

Who doesn't look happy that the Wooden Horse is being pulled into the city?

Things to do

Each one of these six activities is related to one of the pictures in this book. Before you start, look back at the painting to help you remember all about it.

Tobias and the Angel

Draw your own picture of the monstrous fish that attacked and nearly ate Tobias. Think about its huge mouth full of sharp teeth, its glaring eyes, its slimy scales and its spiky fins and tail.

Apollo and Daphne

Draw a picture of how you would imagine Daphne to look when she had been partly transformed into a tree. Think about leaves for hair, branches for fingers and gnarled roots for feet.

Bacchus and Ariadne

Are these statements about the picture of Bacchus and Ariadne on page 14 true or false?

1. Bacchus' chariot is being pulled by two tigers.
2. The satyr is half-pig and half-man.
3. There are two women playing the cymbals.
4. Ariadne is wearing a yellow sash.
5. Bacchus is wearing vine leaves in his hair.
6. There is a very drunk man riding a horse.

Ulysses deriding Polyphemus

Draw how you would imagine Polyphemus,
the one-eyed Cyclops, might look.
Think about how huge and scary
he might be, with his massive,
staring eye in the
middle of his forehead.
Remember that he is
a man-eating giant!

The Capture of the Golden Fleece

Write down the missing words that describe
this picture.

The .... is hanging on the branch of a tree.
It is about to be chopped down by ..... a brave
warrior. A fierce ...... that was guarding it has
been put to sleep by ..... a sorceress, using her
magic ....

In the background you can see Jason's
companions, the ....
Some of them are
unfurling the .....
of their .... getting it
ready to take them
back to Greece.
The soldiers are wearing metal ....
on their heads, and carrying quivers
of ...... and long, sharp ....

The Judgment of Paris

Look back at the picture of Paris and the three
goddesses on page 18. If the people in it could talk,
what might they be saying? Look at their
expressions and gestures to help you write
the conversation they might be having.

Glossary

background
The area in a painting which seems to be farthest away from the viewer. The opposite of foreground.

compose
The way that an artist arranges everything in a picture—people, objects, shapes, and colors.

foreground
The area in a painting which seems to be nearest to the viewer. The opposite of background.

landscape
A painting showing an outdoor view of a real or imaginary place.

mood
The overall feeling of a painting—calm, joyous, threatening, angry, etc.

perspective
A method of drawing or painting spaces, figures, and objects to make them appear three-dimensional.

Renaissance
A French word meaning "rebirth." It is usually applied to the fifteenth and sixteenth centuries, when artists learned, among other things, to apply the rule of perspective.

style
The look of paintings that are typical of either a particular artist or period. An artist's style is one that is recognizable as his or her own.

symbol
An object in a painting that stands for something else. For example, the peacock on page 18 is the symbol that stands for Juno, Queen of all gods and goddesses.

Index

SANGUDO PUBLIC LIBRARY
BOX 524
SANGUDO, AB T0E 2A0